SCHOLASTIC

Success With
Contemporary Cursive

New York • Toronto • London • Auckland • Sydney
Mexico City • New Delhi • Hong Kong • Buenos Aires

Teaching *Resources*

State Standards Correlations

To find out how this book helps you meet your state's standards, log on to **www.scholastic.com/ssw**

Written by Jill Kaufman
Cover design by Ka-Yeon Kim-Li
Interior illustrations by Mark Mason
Interior design by Quack & Company

ISBN-13 978-0-545-20091-2
ISBN-10 0-545-20091-1

4 5 6 7 8 9 10   40   17 16 15 14 13 12

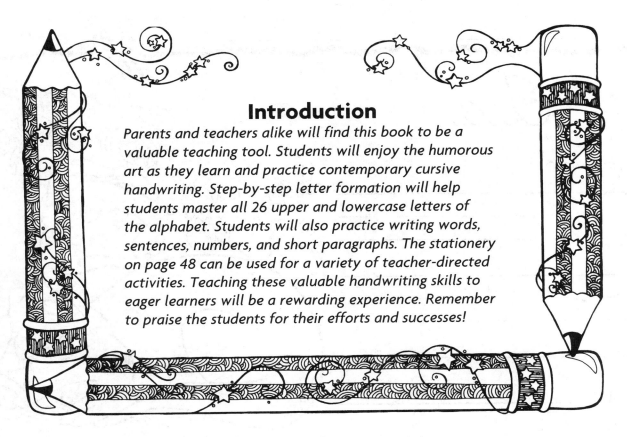

Introduction

Parents and teachers alike will find this book to be a valuable teaching tool. Students will enjoy the humorous art as they learn and practice contemporary cursive handwriting. Step-by-step letter formation will help students master all 26 upper and lowercase letters of the alphabet. Students will also practice writing words, sentences, numbers, and short paragraphs. The stationery on page 48 can be used for a variety of teacher-directed activities. Teaching these valuable handwriting skills to eager learners will be a rewarding experience. Remember to praise the students for their efforts and successes!

Table of Contents

Name _____

Aa

Trace and write.

A A

a a

Aa

Atlantic

ape   apple

Active ants awaken

angry Asian aardvarks.

Bb

Trace and write.

B B

b b

Bb

Baltimore

baby   boy

Beautiful baboons blow

bubbles in a bathtub.

Name _____

Cc

Trace and write.

C C _____

c c _____

Cc _____

Cincinnati _____

candy   case

Confident camels carry

cute, cuddly cats.

_____

_____

6   Scholastic Success With Contemporary Cursive

Dd

Trace and write.

D D

d d

Dd

Detroit

dandy   dirt

Daring dogs decide

to drive to Dallas.

Ee

Trace and write.

E E

e e

Ee

Erie

ever   eye

Elderly, elegant elephants

eagerly eat eggs.

Ff

Trace and write.

$\mathcal{F} \ \mathcal{F}$

$f \ f$

$\mathcal{F}f$

Fenton

five   fast

Frisky foxes frequently

fumble footballs.

Gg

Trace and write.

G G

g g

Gg

Green Bay

gauge   grate

Giggling geese gobble

giant green gumballs.

Hh

Trace and write.

H H H

h h

Hh

Hanover

honor   halt

Happy hamsters have

huge, hilarious hats.

Ii

Trace and write.

I I

i i

Ii

Inglewood

ink   ill

Idle inchworms ignore

irate insects in Iowa.

Name _____

J j

Trace and write.

J J

j j

J j

Joliet

jump   jet

Jaguars juggle jars of

jelly beans in January.

K k

Trace and write.

K K

k k

K k

Kenosha

kite   kick

Kind kangaroos knit

knickers for kids.

Name _____

Ll

Trace and write.

L L

l l

Ll

Littleton

lock   little

Large, lazy lobsters

lounge leisurely.

Mm

Trace and write.

M M

m m

Mm

Missoula

miss   movie

Many merry mice

make mushy meatballs.

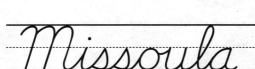

𝒩 𝓃

Trace and write.

𝒩 𝒩

𝓃 𝓃

𝒩 𝓃

Newton

navy   next

Nine nocturnal newts

navigate north nightly.

Oo

Trace and write.

O O

o o

Oo

Omaha

over   oblong

Odorous otters order

olive oil over oysters.

Pp

Trace and write.

P P

p p

Pp

Princeton

pipe   parrot

Pretty pigs pop popcorn

perfectly in Pittsburgh.

𝒬q

Trace and write.

𝒬 𝒬

q q

𝒬q

Quincy

quick   quit

Quaint queens quilt

quickly and quietly.

R r

Trace and write.

R R

r r

R r

Rochester

rich   rear

Restless reindeer run

races rapidly in Reno.

Ss

Trace and write.

S S

s s

Ss

Seattle

sense   safe

Sleepy spiders sell

smelly skunk soap.

SOAP SALE

Tt

Trace and write.

T T T

t t

Tt

Texarkana

total   tea

Talented, toothy toads

teach talkative turtles.

Jump

$\mathcal{U}u$

Trace and write.

$\mathcal{U}\ \mathcal{U}$

$u\ u$

$\mathcal{U}u$

$\mathcal{U}rbana$

$utter$ use

$\mathcal{U}niformed\ umpires$

$usher\ upset\ unicorns.$

$\mathcal{V}v$

Trace and write.

$\mathcal{V}$ $\mathcal{V}$

v v

$\mathcal{V}v$

Vancouver

vivid   vase

Vain vultures

vacuum vigorously.

$\mathcal{W}w$

Trace and write.

$\mathcal{W}\ \mathcal{W}$

$w\ w$

$\mathcal{W}w$

$\mathcal{W}estover$

$women \qquad\qquad wow$

$\mathcal{W}iggly\ worms\ wander$

$westward\ with\ whistles.$

Xx

Trace and write.

X X

x x

Xx

Xenia

axis   exit

Xavier Ox x-rayed

six extra xylophones.

Name _____

Y y

Trace and write.

Y Y

y y

Y y

Yorktown

yacht   yet

Youthful yaks yell.

"Yeah, yellow yo-yos!"

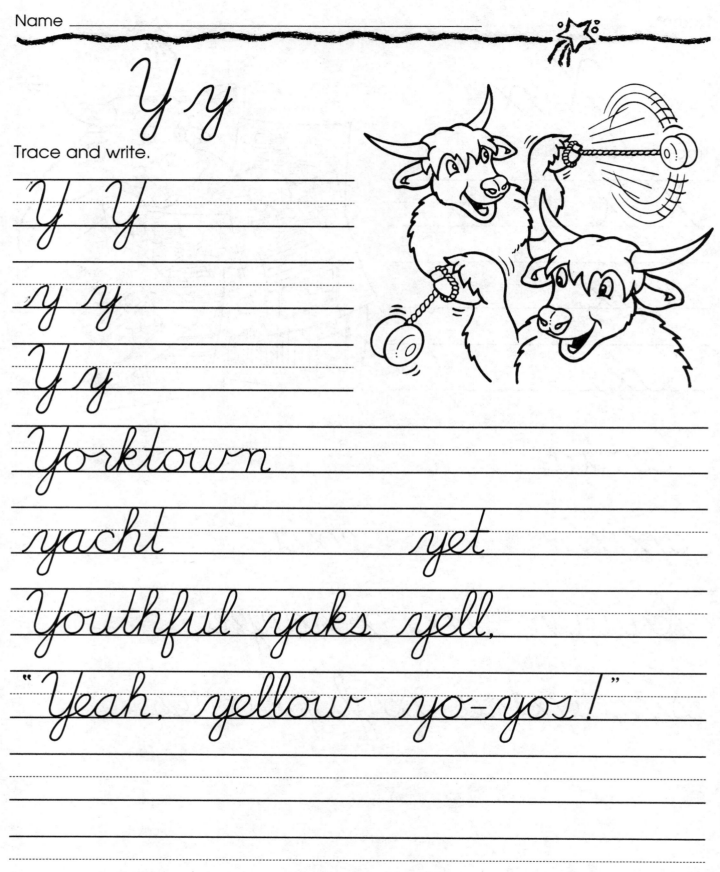

Z Z

Trace and write.

Z Z

Z Z

Z Z

Zanesville

zipper   zero

Zany zebras zigzag

zestfully to Zimbabwe.

Name _____

A-z

A B C D E F G

H I J K L M

N O P 2 R S T

U V W X Y Z

Write.

_____
- -
_____

_____
- -
_____

_____
- -
_____

_____
- -
_____

a - z

a b c d e f g

h i j k l m

n o p q r s t

u v w x y z

Write.

_____
- -
_____
- -
_____
- -
_____
- -
_____

Numbers 0-9

Trace and write.

$0 \quad 0 \quad 0$ _____

$1 \quad 1 \quad 1$ _____

$2 \quad 2 \quad 2$ _____

$3 \quad 3 \quad 3$ _____

$4 \quad 4 \quad 4$ _____

$5 \quad 5 \quad 5$ _____

$6 \quad 6 \quad 6$ _____

$7 \quad 7 \quad 7$ _____

$8 \quad 8 \quad 8$ _____

$9 \quad 9 \quad 9$ _____

 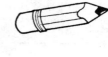   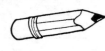

Our Solar System

The sun is the center of our solar system. It is the only star in our solar system. The nine planets and their moons all orbit the sun. The sun provides heat and light to the planets and their moons.

Write.

_____
_____
_____
_____
_____
_____
_____
_____
_____
_____
_____
_____

Ancient Astronomers

People who study the sun, moon, planets, and stars are called astronomers. Cave people were some of the first astronomers. They drew the different shapes of the moon on walls of their caves. Long ago, sailors studied the stars to help them travel. The ancient Greeks discovered many of the planets.

Write.

_____

_____

_____

_____

_____

_____

_____

_____

_____

_____

Name _____

What Is a Year?

A year is the time it takes for a planet to orbit the sun. A year on Earth is 365 days. It only takes Mercury 88 days to make a trip around the sun. However, it takes Uranus 84 Earth years and Pluto 248 Earth years to orbit the sun one time.

Write.

From Hot to Cold

Some planets are so hot or so cold that people cannot live on them. Some days it is 750°F on Mercury. On Venus, the temperature is nearly 900°F! The temperature on Uranus and Neptune is about -350°F. Earth's highest recorded temperature is 136°F and the lowest is -127°F.

Write.

_____

_____

_____

_____

_____

_____

_____

_____

_____

_____

_____

_____

How Many Moons?

In our solar system, scientists have named over 60 moons. Saturn has 18 named moons. Jupiter has 16 moons, and Earth has only one. Some scientists believe Pluto was one of Neptune's moons that escaped from its orbit!

Write.

_____

_____

_____

_____

_____

_____

_____

_____

_____

_____

_____

_____

Speedy Mercury

Mercury is the planet that is closest to the sun. It spins slowly, but it moves around the sun very quickly. Mercury was named after the speedy Roman messenger for the gods.

Write.

_____
_____
_____
_____
_____
_____
_____
_____
_____
_____
_____
_____
_____
_____

Beautiful Venus

Venus is the easiest planet to see
in the sky because it is the closest
to Earth. It is sometimes called the
Evening Star. The Romans named Venus after
their goddess of love and beauty. Venus is so
hot, it could melt lead. It has an orange sky.

Write.

Our Incredible Earth

Earth is the only planet known to have life. It is the right distance from the sun to give it the perfect temperature to have water in all three forms—liquid, vapor, and ice. Although 70 percent of Earth's surface is water, its name means "soil."

Write.

_____

_____

_____

_____

_____

_____

_____

_____

Mysterious Mars

Has there ever been life on Mars?
That remains a mystery. Scientists are
studying the possibility of past, present, or future
life there. Mars is often called the Red Planet
because the rocks on its surface look like rust.
Mars was named after the Roman god of war.

Write.

_____
_____
_____
_____
_____
_____
_____
_____
_____
_____
_____
_____
_____
_____
_____

Sensational Saturn

Saturn is the second largest planet in our solar system. It is most famous for its seven rings made of glittering pieces of ice. Saturn was named after the Roman god of agriculture.

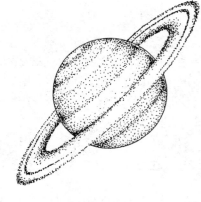

Write.

_____

_____

_____

_____

_____

_____

_____

_____

_____

_____

_____

King Jupiter

Jupiter is the largest planet.
It is so big that 1,300 Earths could
fit inside of it! That is why the
Romans named it after the king
of the Roman gods. Jupiter spins
faster than all the other planets.

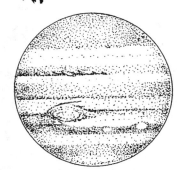

Write.

Understanding Uranus

How can anyone understand very much about a planet nearly two billion miles away? Uranus was the first planet to be discovered through a telescope. It was named after the Roman god who was Saturn's father.

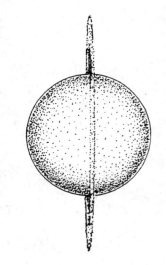

Write.

Not Much About Neptune

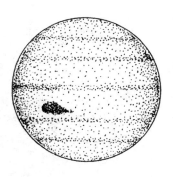

Neptune is difficult to see even
if you have a telescope. It is nearly
three billion miles from the sun.
Neptune takes 165 Earth years to orbit
the sun once. Neptune was named
after the Roman god of the sea.

Write.

Where's Pluto?

Pluto, the smallest planet, is far, far away from the sun—3,666,200,000 miles! Pluto's orbit crosses Neptune's every 248 years. When that happens, Neptune is farther from the sun than Pluto.

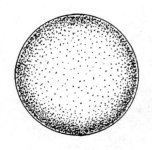

Write.

_____

_____

_____

_____

_____

_____

_____

_____

_____

_____

_____

_____

Name _____

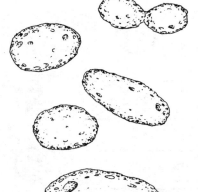

Flying Rocks

Between Mars and Jupiter are chunks of rock that circle the sun. There are thousands and thousands of these flying rocks called asteroids. Asteroids come in many shapes and sizes. Some even look like potatoes!

Write.

_____

_____

_____

_____

_____

_____

_____

_____

_____